Need to Know

Teenage Pregnancy

Mary Nolan

Heinemann
LIBRARY

www.heinemann.co.uk
visit our website to find out more information about **Heinemann Library** books.

To order:
☎ Phone 44 (0) 1865 888066
🖹 Send a fax to 44 (0) 1865 314091
💻 Visit the Heinemann Bookshop at www.heinemann.co.uk to browse our catalogue and order online.

First published in Great Britain by Heinemann Library, Halley Court, Jordan Hill, Oxford OX2 8EJ,
a division of Reed Educational and Professional Publishing Ltd.
Heinemann is a registered trademark of Reed Educational & Professional Publishing Ltd.

Oxford Melbourne Auckland Johannesburg Blantyre Gaborone Ibadan Portsmouth NH (USA) Chicago

© Reed Educational and Professional Publishing Ltd 2002.
The moral right of the proprietor has been asserted.

Designed by M2 Graphic Design
Illustrations by Catherine Ward, except p.37 by Jeff Edwards.
Originated by Ambassador Litho Ltd
Printed in China by South China Printers

ISBN 0431 097984

06 05 04 03 02
10 9 8 7 6 5 4 3 2 1

British Library Cataloguing in Publication Data
Mary Nolan
Teenage Pregnancy – (Need to know)
1.Teenage Pregnancy – Juvenile literature
I Title
618.02'00835

Acknowledgements
The Publishers would like to thank the following for permission to reproduce photographs: Bubbles Photo
Library pp11, 16, 25, 36, 40-41, 45, Corbis pp5, 7, 13, 33, Corbis Stock Market pp12, 20, Imagebank pp8,
19, National Health Service p43, Robert Harding Picture Library pp46, 50, 51, Science Photo library pp9, 10,
14, 17, 23, 39, 42, 64, Stone pp27, 38, 49, 50, Tudor Photography pp15, 34–35.

Graph on page 6 taken from The Alan Guttmacher Institute web site.

Cover photograph reproduced with permission of Wellcome Photo Library.

Every effort has been made to contact copyright holders of any material reproduced in this book. Any
omissions will be rectified in subsequent printings if notice is given to the publisher.

Contents

Any words appearing in the text in bold, **like this**, are explained in the Glossary.

Teenage pregnancy

Every year, thousands of babies are born to teenage parents. In the UK, nearly 8000 girls under the age of 16 and about 2200 under the age of 14 become pregnant. The UK has more teenage pregnancies than any other Western-European country. In Queensland, Australia in 1998 women aged fifteen to nineteen were nearly three times more likely than other women to have babies.

Too young to be a parent?

Although teenagers can be just as loving as older adults towards babies and children, it can be hard for them, as parents, to give their child emotional and financial security. Some teenagers are in stable relationships. Even so, they are still growing up and rather than being ready to give attention, they want lots of attention themselves. They have needs of their own which are very hard to put aside in order to respond 24 hours-a-day to a baby's needs.

A young woman who becomes pregnant may have a more difficult pregnancy than an older woman. She is more likely to have high blood pressure, which can be dangerous both for her and her baby. She is more likely to go into **labour** too early and have a **premature baby** who is underweight. Small babies are more prone to breathing difficulties and they are more at risk of **cot death**.

In some societies, young mothers and fathers are well looked after and are shown how to care for their babies. There are people around who will watch the baby for them and give them a break. Material things are less important, so there's no pressure to provide lots of expensive items for the baby.

In Western societies, young parents are often given a hard time. They can be accused of being irresponsible, selfish, careless and immature. The governments of some countries are not prepared to give much help to young mothers, especially if they are unmarried. Politicians often condemn teenage pregnancies. Voters may not like to see their taxes being spent on supporting young parents. This is not to say that there aren't benefits – just that it can be hard to find out what they are and how to claim them. The best people to ask are midwives and social workers, or one of the organizations listed at the end of this book.

For all these reasons, it's hard to be a teenage parent. Many young people who become parents wish they had waited until they were older. It can be difficult to say 'no' to sex when friends think sleeping around is 'cool', but having sex at an early age places young people at risk, not only of pregnancy, but also of **sexually transmitted diseases** and cancer of the **cervix**.

"It's very easy to get pregnant, but it's ever so hard to be a parent."

(Laura, aged 17)

Young parents

In Shakespeare's play, *Romeo and Juliet*, the heroine, Juliet, is about fourteen years old. Yet all the other characters in the play seem to think that she is quite old enough to be married and have babies. In the past, it was the norm for girls to start childbearing at a very early age. Life expectancy was much shorter than it is today. Many babies did not survive infancy, so women had very large families in the hope that a few children would grow to adulthood. For these reasons, it made sense for couples to start their families at a young age. People tended to live in family groups, or small communities, where there was plenty of support for parents and plenty of willing hands to help out with the children. So being young and a mother or father wasn't nearly as difficult as it is today.

Nowadays, people expect to live well into their seventies and beyond. Better sanitation, housing and health care mean that the majority of babies grow up into healthy children and adults. So there's not the same need to start a family early. Why then do so many teenage girls become pregnant?

One reason is linked to a lack of confidence. Young women may not feel able to ask their boyfriend to use a **condom**. They don't carry condoms around with them in case they're labelled as 'slags', 'scrubbers' or 'easy'.

It won't happen to me

Probably the single most important reason is the feeling that 'it will never happen to me': 'We didn't use a condom. It was my first time. I didn't think you could catch the first time' (Janine, aged 14).

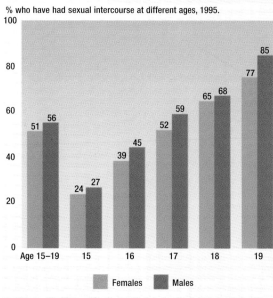

% who have had sexual intercourse at different ages, 1995.

Although this graph shows that only a small percentage of 15 and 16 year-olds are having sex, it doesn't show how often this has resulted in a pregnancy.

Pressures on the young

Media and **peer-group** pressures are enormous. Television, magazines and newspapers are full of stories and pictures about sex, and there's lots of sex-talk amongst teenagers. It's easy for young women and men to feel that perhaps they're the only ones not sleeping with their boyfriend or girlfriend. People might be rushed into sexual relationships before they're really ready.

In fact, figures show that two thirds of teenagers are still virgins when they reach their sixteenth birthday. About one in five young people do not have **sexual intercourse** until they are in their twenties. Men and women who wait until they are older generally enjoy sex more. It's not necessary to be having sex to have a good social life!

Despite her sexy image, Britney Spears has become a role model for young people who don't believe in having sex before marriage.

Sex and drugs

The influence of drugs

Drugs are rife in today's society. People turn to drugs, whether legal or illegal, as a way of solving their problems. The most widely used, and perhaps the most dangerous of all drugs, is alcohol. Young people (like older people) use alcohol because it helps them relax or it makes them feel less depressed (because they meet their friends in a pub) or because they are the children of parents who abuse alcohol. There is a strong relationship between alcohol abuse and teenage pregnancy.

Other drugs such as cocaine, crack cocaine, marijuana and stimulants may be used by young people who want to find out what a 'high' is like, or who are part of a group that regularly uses street drugs. The drugs may make them feel good about themselves, but they also cut them off from reality. Feeling that they can take on the world may lead a person into unsafe sexual behaviour.

❝I was stoned. I didn't know where I was or what I was doing. We had sex in the back of the car. The next day I just knew I was pregnant.❞ (Alex, aged 15)

Sexual abuse

Pregnancy in very young people is sometimes the result of **abusive relationships** in which a girl is forced to have sex against her will by her father, stepfather, mother's boyfriend or another male relative. 'My stepfather has been abusing me for three years. I got pregnant a while ago and he hit me when I told him. He said I had to have an **abortion** or he'd throw me out' (Lauren, aged 15).

Some young people come from families where women are dominated by men. For these women, it can be extremely difficult to say 'no' if a man asks them to have sex. Sexual abuse saps a young woman's self-esteem. She may react by sleeping around because she feels she's not worth anything anyway.

Organizations that can help young people in abusive relationships are listed at the end of this book.

Taking drugs can lead to unsafe sexual behaviour.

Baby challenges

Babies have a wonderful capacity to give love and there are lots of magic moments in the lives of parents with small children. However being a parent isn't plain sailing. Babies born to very young mothers may have a poorer start in life than the babies of older women. They are more likely to:

- be born too early
- have breathing problems
- have infections during their first years of life
- be at risk of **cot death**.

During the first months of a baby's life, it's hard to get a good night's sleep. New parents can feel very isolated because friends who rushed to see the baby when he first came home, don't come so regularly after a while. Mothers have to accept that, for some time, their body is not what it used to be – for example, they may have enlarged breasts, a saggy tummy and lifeless hair. Fathers have to accept that their partner's attention is now divided between them and the baby.

Young parents also have decisions to make about whether, and how, they are going to continue with their education.

Teenage mums are more likely to have premature babies.

While governments try to ensure that educational opportunities are available for teenage parents, it can be hard to go back to studying after the momentous events of pregnancy and birth.

Girls who get pregnant at an early age often do less well at school, gain fewer qualifications and have poorer job prospects than their friends whose education wasn't interrupted by a baby. They may have to live on benefits which are just enough to feed, clothe and house them, but not enough to have a really good time.

Some young people say that their baby makes up for the things they have lost: 'I spend all my time with my baby. Just having her around is enough for me. I don't envy my friends who've gone to college' (Claire, aged 16).

Others feel that they are missing out: 'If I could go back, I'd definitely wait to get pregnant. There's so much I wanted to do, but I'm tied down by the baby now.' (Cherri, aged 17).

Babies need lots of attention. Even older parents sometimes find it hard to cope.

OK to be pregnant?

Some cultures are very accepting of young parents. For them, a girl who has a couple of children by the time she is eighteen is simply doing what her mother and grandmother did before her. She might be part of a supportive, caring community and have friends embarking on motherhood at the same time as herself. She may well enjoy mothering her babies and not feel that she has missed out on her youth.

Family support can be very important for all mothers — however young or old they are.

Pregnancy is a time when women receive a lot of attention from a whole range of health and social-care professionals. This can provide an opportunity to sort out a drug problem, an **abusive relationship** or other financial, social or educational difficulties. It's easier for a girl to ask for help when she knows that the well-being of her baby depends on sorting herself out. 'I'd never had the will-power to stop drinking until I got pregnant. The baby made me stop, with a lot of help from my midwife' (Helena, aged 16).

Pregnancy may draw a young woman back into her family and re-establish a relationship with her parents that was

previously at breaking point. Some families are very good at rallying round when there is a crisis to face. However, more families are torn apart by teenage pregnancy than are brought together.

Some young women are thrown out of their homes when they tell their parents they are pregnant. The parents feel ashamed. They are worried about what their relatives and neighbours will say. They may have jobs where it will be difficult for them to admit that their teenage daughter is going to have a baby. They may feel that all their hopes for the future of their daughter have been dashed.

Some young women are desperate for love and they feel that a baby will love them as they have never been loved before. It is tragic that anyone should feel the need to get pregnant for this reason. It should be remembered that, at least initially, babies take much more love than they give and that small children can be very challenging as well as affectionate.

Pregnancy – finding out

Nowadays, pregnancy tests are very sophisticated. They can tell a woman that she is pregnant very soon after she has conceived a baby. However, there are plenty of natural signs that pregnancy is underway. The most obvious is missing a **period**. Even before this happens, a woman may become aware that her breasts feel very full and tingly, perhaps even painful. Her tummy feels full, although her baby is still tiny. She may feel very tired because her body is busy reorganizing her **circulation** and her digestion to cope with supporting two lives instead of one.

The baby is growing from hour to hour, developing incredibly rapidly from a cluster of cells into a recognizable human being. The result of all this frantic activity is that the pregnant woman often feels drained. Some women start to feel sick at the very beginning of pregnancy and this is the first sign for them that a baby is on the way. Most women say they 'just knew' they were pregnant, even before their bodies started telling them.

**❝I had a gut feeling
I was pregnant.❞**

(Maria, aged 17)

Pregnancy tests

It's helpful for a woman to find out whether she's pregnant as soon as possible. If she is happy to be pregnant, she can start to take special care of herself in order to give her baby the best start in life. If she wants to have an **abortion**, it's safer if the procedure is carried out in the first three months of pregnancy. If she's not sure about the pregnancy, she has time to talk to other people before making any decisions.

Confidential, free pregnancy tests are available from:
- family planning clinics
- Brook advisory centres
- sexual health clinics
- young people's centres.

In Australia, they are available from:
- family planning centres
- student health clinics
- youth services (in some states)
- **GPs**.

Home testing kits can be obtained from pharmacies or drugstores. They're expensive, but easy to use. In the UK, most family doctors (GPs) will carry out a free test for a young woman without insisting on speaking to her parents.

Pregnancy tests involve mixing a few drops of urine with some chemicals to detect the presence or absence of pregnancy **hormones**. They can be used on the day the woman's period should have started, although they are more reliable if carried out a few days after this.

Home pregnancy tests are not difficult to carry out – and give results quickly.

Pregnancy – finding out

Testing positive

All women feel a strong mixture of emotions when they find out that they're pregnant. They might be shocked, amazed, terrified, excited and uncertain all at the same time! Girls who are still at school and not in a steady relationship often feel very scared.

Some young women go into a state of denial when they discover they're pregnant. They ignore the early signs of pregnancy and try to pretend that nothing is happening. They may feel that they've let their parents down and be terrified of telling them the news. They may also be frightened of telling their boyfriend. Weeks can pass while they try to decide what to do next. Some girls continue to conceal their pregnancies until the day the baby is due and give birth on their own, or go to the hospital as an emergency.

It's very risky not to get any help. Young women (just like older women) need emotional support to cope with

"The pregnancy test said I was pregnant, but I didn't believe it. I was throwing up all the time but I refused to believe it."

(Leanne, aged 15)

pregnancy and physical care to make sure that they keep well. Although pregnancy is a healthy experience for most women, things do occasionally go wrong – placing the life of both mother and child in jeopardy.

So it's important to talk to someone. Parents are sometimes unexpectedly supportive once they've got over the initial shock. 'Instead of being angry, my Dad stood there, hugging me...he added that he'd stick by me whatever I did' (Lois, aged 17).

Other people to talk to are:
- a doctor
- a youth worker
- a school nurse
- a favourite teacher
- an adult friend.

A trusted adult can help the girl break the news to her parents or other important people in her life. 'I told my English tutor. She was great. She said I had to tell my parents, but she came with me' (Mylene, aged 16).

Finding out you're pregnant is easier if there's someone to support you.

Becoming a father

A young man is likely to be every bit as shocked by the news that his girlfriend is pregnant as she is herself. He may be delighted and feel that he will be more respected by his friends. Or he may be terrified at the thought of how difficult it will be to be a father while he is still at school, or in a low-paid job. Some young men are very angry and feel their girlfriend has cheated on them. 'She told me she was on the pill and then she got pregnant. She really landed me in it' (Lewis, aged 17).

It can be just as hard for a young man to tell his parents that he has got someone 'in trouble' as it is for a young woman to tell her parents. He needs as much support as she does to handle the situation. Many boys and young men find it very difficult to express their feelings. Trying to find the right words to talk to their girlfriend may prove impossible. It is often easier simply to refuse to speak to her again. The relationship can come to an end with both partners feeling angry and distressed.

Fathers

Sometimes a boy is contacted months after sleeping with a girl and told that he is the father of her baby. While he may be prepared to shoulder his responsibilities, he still wants to be certain that the baby is his. A **DNA** test after the baby is born may be the only way of solving this problem.

Research shows that the fathers of babies born to teenagers under 16 are, in general, 5 or more years older than the mother. If the teenage girl is under the age of consent (16 in the UK, 17 in South Australia and Tasmania and 16 in other Australian states) the father might be frightened of being prosecuted for having sex with an underage girl. In the UK and Australia, if a boy is named as the father on the baby's birth certificate, he will be contacted and required to contribute to the financial upkeep of his child.

There is a list of organizations, at the end of this book, that offer advice and support to fathers of all ages.

> **"I knew my parents would go mad. And they did. And I still had to face my girlfriend's parents."**
>
> (Mark, aged 16)

Choosing an abortion

Sometimes a woman will decide not to continue with her pregnancy. The decision to end a pregnancy is always a tough one. Even if a girl is quite sure that she doesn't want a baby, an **abortion** is likely to have a profound impact on her. Women who have ended their pregnancies often think about the babies they chose not to have for years afterwards. The babies they eventually have do not replace the ones they've lost: they're simply different babies. Any young woman considering an abortion should receive counselling from a qualified nurse, youth or social worker.

It is important to talk things through before deciding on an abortion.

An abortion can be a hazardous procedure if it isn't carried out in a hospital or at a properly registered clinic. Every year, 'back street abortions' lead to serious infections and sometimes death for many women in different parts of the world.

Before the operation can go ahead, two doctors have to agree that an abortion is necessary to protect the physical and/or mental well-being of the mother. Abortions are usually carried out before 14 weeks of pregnancy, although they can be carried out as late as 24 weeks in the UK, and 28 weeks in Australia.

Abortion before fourteen weeks

If the pregnancy is less than nine weeks, it can be terminated by using an abortion pill and gel which is put into the **vagina** to make the **womb** contract and expel the **foetus**. A girl who is more than nine weeks pregnant, but less than fourteen weeks, is admitted to hospital as a day case (there is no need for an overnight stay). The abortion is carried out in an operating theatre under **general anaesthetic**. The surgeon stretches the neck of the womb and then scrapes out the contents – the foetus and the **placenta**. Following the operation, specially trained nurses monitor the girl to make sure that she is not bleeding heavily.

Having a sympathetic person to talk to in the days after the abortion is very important. 'I was so relieved when I woke up after the operation. I felt great – everything was going to be OK. I could get on with my life. But a couple of days later, it really hit me what I'd done. And I was very sad for a long while after that, thinking about my baby' (Carla, aged 14).

Choosing an abortion

Late abortion

There are two ways of ending a pregnancy that has progressed beyond fourteen weeks. A medical **abortion** is when drugs are used to make the woman's body go into **labour** and push the baby out of the **womb**. The drugs may be given in the form of **pessaries** which are placed high up in the **vagina**, or through a drip. Going into labour when there's not going to be a living baby at the end is a traumatic experience. Once the womb starts to contract, the abortion can be very painful and doctors generally prescribe strong pain-relieving drugs to keep the woman comfortable. A nurse stays with her all the time and she can have a friend with her.

At some hospitals, late abortions are carried out as a surgical procedure. The neck of the womb is stretched open and the baby is cut out. The thought of this is very distressing to some women and they prefer to go to a hospital or clinic which offers medical abortion.

In Australia, a teenage girl can give her consent to an abortion. In the UK, a girl who is over 16 can consent. A girl who is younger will usually need the consent of one of her parents, her guardian or social worker. Depending on her relationship with the father of the baby, she might want to ask his opinion, but he cannot prevent her from having an abortion.

Once a pregnancy has progressed beyond 14 weeks, the abortion procedure becomes more difficult and distressing.

Molly's story

'I was 15 when I got pregnant and I was living with foster carers. I knew straightaway that I couldn't keep the baby, but I was four months gone before I told my social worker. She felt I was right to have an abortion and she said there was no need to tell my parents because I'd had a lot of trouble with my dad in the past and my mum always supported him. The abortion took about ten hours, but I didn't have any pain because of all the drugs they gave me. I saw the baby when it was born – just quickly. I think I made the right decision to have the abortion, but next time I get pregnant, it has to be for keeps.'

Adoption and fostering

Some young women do not agree with **abortion** or they feel that they could not put themselves through the stress of terminating their pregnancy. However, they know that they haven't got the emotional or financial resources to cope with a baby. For them, adoption is a possibility.

Adoption is a big decision. The mother will need counselling and the support of a social worker to help her think through the pros and cons very carefully. Once the adoption has gone through the courts, she will no longer be the legal parent of her child. A father cannot prevent his baby from being adopted if he is not married to the mother. However, a social worker will contact him to ask his opinion, unless the mother feels that she cannot say who the father is.

Difficult decisions

It's impossible to make a definite decision about adoption until after the baby is born. Pregnancy is a time of tumultuous feelings; birth is a major life event. Only after the birth can a mother be really sure of her feelings.

A girl considering adoption can see her baby after she has given birth. She can hold him and spend some time with him. It seems to be easier to cope with the grief of giving up a baby if the mother has a picture in her mind of the person for whom she is grieving.

The baby then goes to a foster home where the birth mother can see him as often as she likes. She can also be involved in choosing an adoptive family.

Occasionally, adopters are happy for the birth mother to continue to see her baby. Others are prepared to send an annual report with photographs of the child, but do not want any face-to-face contact. Some birth mothers do not wish to see their child again, preferring a clean break.

Fostering is an alternative to adoption. A member of the birth mother's own family might foster the baby until the mother is ready to look after him herself. She remains the legal parent. A girl who is under 18 can be fostered together with her baby.

Birth parents can sometimes keep in touch with their adopted children. Sometimes they receive photographs or other momentos or reminders of their child.

Keeping the baby

Many young women have strong views about **abortion**, but would find it too difficult to give up their baby for adoption. So they decide to keep their baby. This isn't an easy decision and there are a number of factors that are likely to influence its success.

Firstly, the mother needs support during pregnancy and after the birth, preferably from adults with an understanding of what life is like with a young child. Some young fathers are prepared to support their partners emotionally, even if they are unable to make a financial contribution. Often, however, relationships break up during the young woman's pregnancy or shortly after the birth of the baby: 'I wasn't ready for fatherhood. I couldn't cope with being tied down, and my girlfriend changed when she had the baby. She didn't want me as much' (Josh, aged 17).

Financial security

Financial security is essential and if the mother's family can't help her, she needs to apply for benefits. Benefits can be a minefield, especially for young people under 16 years of age as they are not able to apply for them themselves. Social workers and youth workers can help with filling in forms.

Most importantly, the young mother needs to consider how having a baby will affect her life over the next few years. She needs to think about whether she will continue her education, where she can find help with the baby and how she can improve her job prospects. As soon as possible, she should register for maternity care and decide whether she wants to give birth to the baby in hospital or at home. Then there are clothes and nappies to be bought and basic equipment such as a cot, car seat and pushchair.

There's a lot to think about at a time when the girl's body is going through tremendous changes and her emotions can be very confused. This is why having someone to talk to whom she trusts and respects is so important.

"I don't think I could have managed without my mum. She was brilliant – kept me sane, really."

(Adrianna, aged 17)

Being pregnant

A normal pregnancy can last from 37 to 42 weeks. To find out when the baby might be due, the doctor adds nine months and seven days to the date on which the girl's last **period** started. For example:

First day of last period	Baby due
January 14th	October 21st
June 7th	March 14th
September 3rd	June 10th

This is called the Estimated Date of Delivery or Expected Date of Delivery (EDD), but it is only an estimation, a rough guide to when the baby might be born.

Doctors and midwives divide pregnancy into three sections, called **trimesters**. Each trimester covers three months. In the first trimester, pregnant women tend to be tired and rather unpredictable – happy one minute and depressed the next. The woman's body is being totally reorganized to look after her unborn baby. She may find that her appetite changes so that she no longer wants foods that she used to enjoy and that other foods become favourites. Many women go off coffee and tea during pregnancy, which is just as well as caffeine is not particularly good for the baby.

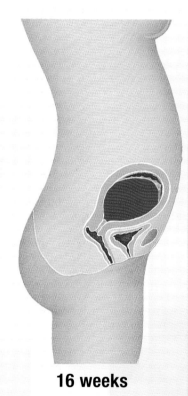

The pregnancy is just beginning to show.

16 weeks

During the second trimester, the pregnant woman generally feels much more positive. Her energy levels pick up and at about 20 weeks, she can at last start to feel her baby making tiny fluttering movements inside her. Her tummy starts to swell and other people notice that she's pregnant and make a fuss of her. By 26 weeks, the baby is moving quite vigorously and the top of her 'bump' is above her belly button.

In the third trimester, the weight of the baby can make being pregnant very uncomfortable. Back-ache is common, and so are swollen ankles and aching legs because the woman's heavy belly gets in the way of the circulation to her legs. Finding a comfortable position for sleeping isn't easy. Sleep can be further disturbed by the need to go to the toilet frequently because the baby is pressing down on the **bladder**. As the mother's EDD approaches, she can start to feel very apprehensive about the labour, as well as excited at the prospect of seeing her baby. 'By nine months, I was fed up with being pregnant. I just wanted to see the baby' (Kim, aged 15).

Maternity clothes are definitely needed now!

28 weeks

Being so large is exhausting.

36 weeks

Being pregnant

The baby inside

The first three months of pregnancy are when the baby is growing most rapidly. As early as six weeks after conception, its heart can be seen beating on an **ultrasound scan**. By twelve weeks, his or her kidneys are fully functional and are making urine. Blood is circulating around the body; the baby can suck and swallow and it is possible to detect his or her sex organs.

From twelve to twenty weeks, the baby's skeleton takes shape. The nose forms and the two parts of the palate of the mouth join together. The skin becomes covered with soft downy hair called **lanugo** and fingernails start to grow. The baby moves more and more vigorously so that by twenty weeks, the mother can feel him or her wriggling inside her.

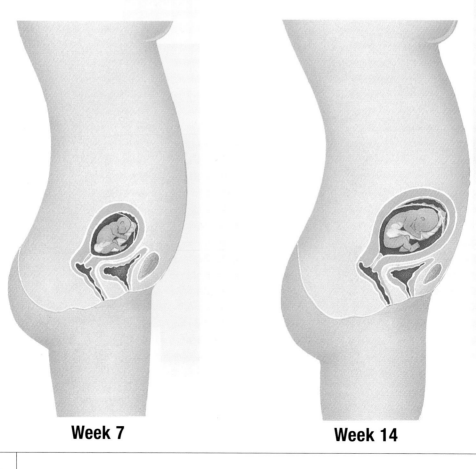

Week 7   **Week 14**

Half-way through

Half-way through the pregnancy, the baby starts to develop a pattern of sleeping and waking which the mother quickly learns to recognize. The baby can now hear and distinguish between different sounds. By the time he or she is born, the baby is able to recognize his mother's voice. If he or she were to be born at 24 weeks of pregnancy, there would be a small chance of survival. Chances of survival increase with every additional week spent inside the **womb**.

By 28 weeks, the baby's eyelids are open and he or she can distinguish between light and dark. The baby is making shallow breathing movements, exercising lungs ready for birth. In the final twelve weeks of pregnancy, the baby's skin, which has been red and wrinkled, becomes smooth and most of the hair that has covered the body disappears. Stores of fat are laid down which make the face and body rounded. The fat will provide the baby with energy for birth and for the first few days of life when the mother has only small amounts of breast milk to give. The hair on the head and the nails grow rapidly and the bones of the skull become harder.

By the end of pregnancy, nature has carefully prepared him or her for life outside the womb. Unlike most other mammals, however, the child will be highly dependent on the mother for years to come.

Week 30

Towards the end of pregnancy, most babies settle into a head-down position.

Pregnancy life-style

Pregnant women share their lives with their unborn babies in a very intimate way. Whatever they eat and drink, their babies must also eat and drink; if they smoke, their babies have to smoke; if they catch an infection, their babies run the risk of catching it as well. So it's really important for an expectant mother to take care of herself and give her baby a good start in life.

Folic acid

Research has shown that babies are less likely to develop **spina bifida** – a condition that can cause paralysis – if the mother takes extra folic acid while she is pregnant. She needs at least 400 micrograms (0.4 mg) every day for the first 12 weeks of her pregnancy. Although folic acid is present in foods such as dark green leafy vegetables, and is often added to flour, bread and cereals, it's still wise to take a supplement. Supplements can be bought from a pharmacy.

Infections

Infections such as **rubella** and chicken-pox can damage the unborn baby. Pregnant women should also avoid children who are ill, or who have recently been **vaccinated**.

Another source of infection is cat litter which may contain an organism called *Toxoplasma gondii*, which causes **toxoplasmosis** in humans. Pregnant women should always wear gloves to empty a cat litter tray or when gardening, as soil may be contaminated with cat faeces.

Diet

The usual rules of a good diet apply during pregnancy – plenty of fresh fruit and vegetables and plenty of carbohydrates such as bread, pasta and potatoes. Protein is required in moderation in the form of meat, eggs or fish. Vitamins are also important, but tablets should be taken only on the advice of a doctor because too much of certain vitamins can harm the baby. Sweet sugary foods should be kept for special treats – they're not an essential part of a good diet!

There are a few foods to avoid and these include liver, soft cheeses such as brie and camembert, blue-veined cheeses, paté, uncooked meats and raw or lightly boiled eggs. All of these foods may contain harmful bacteria. Pre-prepared meals from the chiller cabinet at the supermarket should not be eaten cold, but only after they have been reheated so that they are piping hot.

It's important to have a really healthy diet during pregnancy with plenty of fresh fruit and vegetables.

Drugs and pregnancy

Many women find it possible to kick problem habits during pregnancy. There are lots of organizations that will help pregnant girls deal with drug, alcohol, tobacco or substance abuse. Some are listed at the end of this book.

Experts disagree on how much alcohol it is safe to drink during pregnancy, but everyone is certain that binge-drinking should be avoided. It seems wisest for pregnant women to give up alcohol altogether, or drink just a few units a week – perhaps one or two glasses of wine.

Smoking has been shown to stunt the growth of unborn babies. Some girls think that a smaller baby will make giving birth easier, but this simply isn't true. Also, underweight babies are at risk of breathing and other health problems. It's never too late to give up smoking, even if the pregnancy is well advanced. Every day without cigarettes reduces the likelihood that the mother will have a **miscarriage** or go into **labour** prematurely, and improves the baby's chances of being healthy. 'When I got pregnant, I thought, "If I can't give up smoking now, I never will." But it was terribly hard. My boyfriend kept me going' (Rosie, aged 15).

There is insufficient research to say whether cannabis is harmful during pregnancy, although some people think that it may predispose the baby to cancer. Snorting, smoking or injecting cocaine during pregnancy has very serious consequences. Babies born to cocaine-addicted mothers are irritable and jumpy, impossible to cuddle and difficult to feed.

It's not safe to take even over-the-counter drugs without checking first with a doctor. The **thalidomide** tragedy of the 1960s has made everyone aware of the possible harmful effects of any drug on an unborn baby.

Exercise

Young women often use alcohol, tobacco and street drugs to help them relax. There are all sorts of other ways of relaxing, however, which are far healthier – taking exercise, for example. It's perfectly safe to start a gentle exercise programme during pregnancy as long as it isn't so vigorous that it causes sickness or exhaustion. Walking and swimming are especially good forms of exercise to get fit for labour.

No one's sure how much it's safe to drink during pregnancy. Cut out alcohol altogether or stick to one or two drinks a week.

Pregnancy care

In the UK, pregnancy care is provided by midwives, **GPs** (family doctors) and obstetricians (doctors specializing in pregnancy and childbirth). Most women receive some of their care from each of these professionals.

There are a number of routine checks that take place each time pregnant women go to the pregnancy clinic.

- Their blood pressure is checked. This is very important because high blood pressure reduces the efficiency of the **placenta** and puts the baby at risk.
- Their urine is tested for sugar and protein. Some women develop **diabetes** during pregnancy and this means that they need to be cared for by a doctor who specializes in diabetes. Protein in the urine often goes with high blood pressure, and is a warning sign that there may be problems with the pregnancy.
- The distance from the top of the **womb** to the pubic hairline is measured. The number of centimetres corresponds to the number of weeks of pregnancy (that is, 20 cm = 20 weeks pregnant).
- The baby is palpated, which means that the doctor or midwife feels the baby through the abdomen to check on his size and find out his position in the womb.

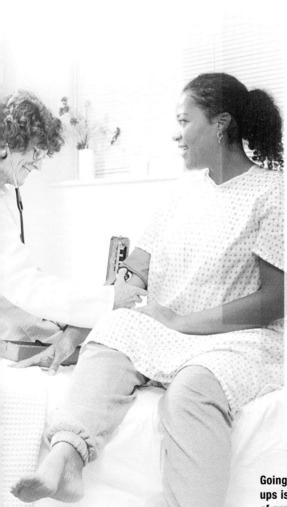

Going for regular check-ups is an important part of pregnancy.

Various blood tests are also carried out during pregnancy. These are to find out the woman's blood group, whether she is **Rhesus** positive or negative, whether she has **sickle cell disease** or **thalassaemia** and whether she is **anaemic**.

At every clinic visit, the mother should be given the opportunity to discuss her worries in confidence. Health professionals are trained to be non-judgmental. This is the time to talk about smoking, drug or substance abuse and violent relationships as well as any other problems. Some young women might want to be checked for **sexually transmitted diseases** such as gonorrhoea, which can cause premature **labour** if not treated. Specially trained nurses are available to offer **HIV** counselling.

Many women take their partner with them to the pregnancy clinic, or someone else to keep them company and help them ask the questions they want answering.

❝❝I was frightened to ask questions in case I said something stupid. My social worker came with me and she found out the things I wanted to know.❞❞

(Lisa, aged 14)

As pregnancy goes on, the top of the 'bump' gets higher and higher.

36 weeks ⟶

20 weeks ⟶

12 weeks ⟶

Pregnancy care

Is the baby healthy?

Women (and men) often have vivid dreams during pregnancy about their babies being abnormal in some way. It is natural to worry about whether the baby will be healthy. Some people are particularly worried about having a baby with learning disabilities such as Down's syndrome. Very young women are, in fact, at low risk of giving birth to a baby with Down's, but it does happen.

There are two kinds of test that can be carried out during pregnancy to check the baby's health. **Screening tests** estimate the risk of the baby being abnormal. **Diagnostic tests** can say for certain whether the baby has a problem.

Most women are offered a blood test to screen for **spina bifida** and Down's syndrome between fifteen and eighteen weeks of pregnancy. A negative result means that the baby has only a very small chance of being abnormal. A positive result means that the baby has a higher chance. The results do not mean that the baby either definitely has or definitely hasn't got spina bifida or Down's.

Ultrasound scans can be screening or diagnostic. Sometimes, a scan shows quite clearly that there is a problem with the baby's spine, kidneys or heart. Other times, the scan is inconclusive.

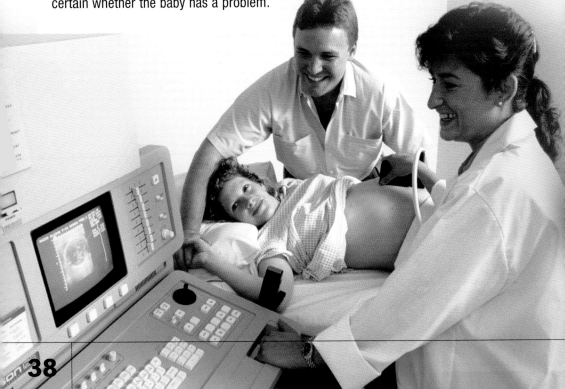

Chorionic villus sampling (CVS) and amniocentesis are diagnostic tests. CVS is carried out at about eleven weeks of pregnancy and amniocentesis at eighteen weeks. The doctor puts a fine needle through the mother's abdomen and takes a small sample of either the **placenta** (CVS) or the **amniotic fluid** (amniocentesis). The medical laboratory analyzes the sample to find out whether the baby is healthy.

Both CVS and amniocentesis carry a 0.5 per cent to 2 per cent risk that the mother will miscarry following the procedure.

If a diagnostic test is positive, the mother has to decide whether she wants to continue with the pregnancy, or choose an **abortion**. Even if she wouldn't have an abortion under any circumstances, she might still want to have a test.

❝I would never have got rid of the baby. But I wanted the tests so that if she had something wrong with her, I'd be prepared.❞

(Becca, aged 17)

Giving birth

Most girls are frightened about giving birth. They wonder how painful **labour** is going to be, and whether they will cope. Having someone to support them, such as their mother, or best friend or the baby's father, helps enormously. Some men are happy to be with their partner during labour, and others are not. No man should feel forced to be present at the birth.

Labour occurs in three stages. The first stage is when the **womb** starts to contract rhythmically and regularly, and the neck of the womb slowly opens until it is 10 cm dilated. This usually takes from eight to eighteen hours. In the second stage of labour, the baby is pushed down the **vagina** by the powerful muscles of the womb and by the mother's pushing. This stage lasts from one to two hours. The **placenta** is delivered in the third stage of labour, which may last just a few minutes or a couple of hours.

Labour increases in intensity over a period of hours. When the contractions become very strong, most women find them painful. If left to their own devices, women will find many ways of helping themselves cope with the pain – changing their position, rocking their hips, rubbing their backs and moaning. These are all natural forms of pain relief. There are also drugs available to help with the pain. These can be very effective, but may have unwanted side effects for both mother and baby.

It's important to have special friends to be there for you in labour.

Giving permission

Giving birth in hospital generally involves various medical procedures. These may be welcomed by the mother or they may leave her feeling out of control. It is important that she gives her permission before any procedure is carried out, and that she is kept fully informed about the progress of her labour and her baby's well-being.

When the baby is born, the mother and father, if he is present, need time together to bond as a new family. Parents enjoy stroking their baby, counting his fingers and toes and holding him skin to skin. 'Soon after she was born, we were left alone. Holding the baby was just amazing. Jon, my partner, cried. She was so beautiful' (Louisa, aged 19).

Is breast best?

A newly born baby needs to be fed milk. Breast milk is definitely best for babies, but breastfeeding may not always be best for mothers. Girls who dislike the idea of breastfeeding will be happier giving their baby bottles, and should not be made to feel guilty about their choice. The father's feelings are very influential. If he is supportive, breastfeeding is much more likely to be successful than if he is not. 'Some of my mates made remarks about my girlfriend breastfeeding. But I didn't want my baby to have bottles. I think breastmilk is the natural thing' (Noel, aged 18).

Breastfeeding has many advantages. Milk is always ready for the baby as soon as he or she is hungry. It comes at the right temperature and costs nothing. As the baby grows, the composition of the breast milk changes to match his or her needs. **Formula milk** is expensive. Bottles have to be **sterilized** and the milk mixed and heated.

Breast milk gives babies the best start in life.

Advantages

Bottle-fed babies are much more likely to be hospitalized during the first seven years of their lives than breastfed babies. Breast milk protects babies against allergies, such as **eczema** and **asthma**, and against ear infections and tummy upsets. Later in life, children who have been breastfed are usually more intelligent, and less at risk of **diabetes**, obesity and other serious diseases such as **multiple sclerosis**. Women who breastfeed are less likely to suffer from breast cancer and **osteoporosis**. They also regain their pre-pregnancy weight more quickly.

Most women know that breast milk is best, but it can be difficult to choose breastfeeding when society tends to see breasts only as sexual objects. Stories of women being asked to leave restaurants and public places because they are breastfeeding illustrate how uncomfortable people are with the natural way of feeding babies. Women need support to breastfeed successfully and some of the organizations that can help are listed at the end of this book. 'I found breastfeeding really difficult to begin with and my mum kept telling me to give up. She said bottles had been good enough for me. But a breastfeeding counsellor helped me and after a few weeks, it was easy and it was lovely' (Claire, aged 16).

Government campaigns encourage mothers to breastfeed their babies.

Life with a baby

What is it like to be a teenage parent? Some teenage parents are married or in a stable relationship. It's more difficult for those who are not:

Nadia (aged 18):

'I split up with my boyfriend when I was five months pregnant. He definitely did not want to be a father. After the baby was born, I went back home to live with my mum. The house was small enough before, but with all the baby stuff, there was no room at all. I was tired for weeks on end. The baby kept waking up in the night, and he wanted attention all day. My mum was great, but she got tired too because she works full time. It took ages to get anything done. Having a shower and dressing took me until the afternoon. Meeting friends was nice but I felt I hadn't much in common with them.'

'After a while, things got easier. Jamie (my baby) started sleeping for longer and I was more organized. It was still hard to have a decent social life. I really missed my freedom. Jamie's three now and my youth worker has found a nursery place for him. I'm starting to think about my future. I want to get some qualifications and find a job so that Jamie and I can have a good life together.'

Sharon (aged 17):

'My parents said I shouldn't see Liam any more after I got pregnant. But we stuck together. He's twenty. He's working and we have a small flat. We want to move to a flat with a garden so that Ellie can play outside. She's nearly two now and she's gorgeous, but it's hard to find time for me and Liam with her around. I'm not sorry I had her, but I'd advise anyone my age to think very carefully about getting pregnant. If you want a baby, fine. But don't end up having one because you couldn't be bothered to use a **condom**.'

Lucy, youth worker:

'To be honest, I'm amazed at how well some young women cope with having a baby. They've got virtually no money and they're living in grotty accommodation, but they survive. They're really strong. But a lot of teenagers find being a parent too hard, especially if they haven't any support. The baby ends up in care. That's very sad; it's not good for the mothers and it's not good for the babies.'

Babies and mums need to get out of the house.

Legal matters

Age of consent

In England, Scotland and Wales, the age at which young people can legally consent to have sex with someone of the opposite sex is 16. In Northern Ireland it is 17. In South Australia and Tasmania it is 17, and in Victoria, New South Wales, Queensland, Australian Capital Territory, Western Australia and the Northern Territory it is 16. If a man has sex with an under-age girl, he risks being prosecuted. The police don't always press charges unless the man is much older than the girl or he has a responsible job, such as a teacher or doctor.

Contraception

A doctor will not tell the parents or guardians of a young person under the age of 16 that he or she has asked for **contraceptive** information. In the UK, contraception is always readily available. However, in some countries the doctor might not agree to prescribe contraceptives. In South Australia, a doctor needs another doctor to agree that the girl is capable of giving informed consent before she can be prescribed contraceptives.

Abortion

In the UK, if a girl is 16 or over, she has the right to consent to an **abortion**. If she is under sixteen, a doctor will normally want consent from her parents or social worker. If the girl feels she cannot confide in her guardians, some doctors might be prepared to go ahead with the abortion without their permission. In Australia, a teenage girl can consent to an abortion as long as her doctor feels that she is sufficiently mature to understand what she is asking for.

Adoption and fostering

The father's consent is not required for adoption if he is not married to the baby's mother. Adoptions are arranged through the courts and cannot be changed once they have been agreed in law. If a child is **fostered**, the mother (and father if they are married) remain the legal parents.

Fathers' rights and responsibilities

The father has no automatic right to be involved in bringing up his baby if he is not married to the mother and if he is not named on the birth registration forms. If he is named, he has some rights and some financial responsibilities. If the mother does not want the father to have access to the baby and he has been named on the birth registration forms, she must go to court and ask for an **injunction**.

Avoiding pregnancy

Taking responsibility for not getting pregnant means using some form of **contraception** or not having sex. Having fun with a boyfriend or girlfriend doesn't necessarily mean making love. Sometimes, sex can spoil a relationship rather than improve it. Young people who wait to have sex until they are in their late teens or early twenties are less at risk of **sexually transmitted diseases** and unwanted pregnancies. They enjoy sex more because they are more confident and more able to make up their own minds about what they want to do and what they don't.

Figures from the USA show that one in four teenage mothers has a second child within two years of her first. For some, the pregnancy is planned, but often it's not. Some people think you can't get pregnant if you have sex in the bath, or if the girl has a shower immediately afterwards, or if she **douches** her **vagina** with vinegar. None of these are true.

It's possible for a girl to become pregnant after having a baby even before her **periods** start again. So it's important to talk to a health professional about contraception before the baby is born.

Condoms

Condoms are the only form of contraception that offer protection against sexually transmitted diseases as well as preventing pregnancy (they are 98 per cent effective). They're easy to buy and can be obtained free from family planning clinics and teen services centres. Clingfilm or plastic wrap do not do the same job as a condom! A girl may find that her vagina is quite dry in the months after she has had a baby. Using a **lubricant** on the condom makes sex easier and is fine as long as it is not oil-based. Body oil or cream may damage the condom and make it more likely to split. A **female condom** is now available that gives 95 per cent protection against pregnancy.

Some girls think that carrying condoms around or going to a clinic to get contraception will make them look like sluts. Some boys think that having a condom in their pocket makes it look as if they are expecting to have sex. However, they are simply behaving responsibly; it's not a question of being 'easy'.

Birth control pill

If a girl is breastfeeding and she wants to go back on the pill, she will be prescribed the 'minipill' which does not have any harmful effects on her baby. It is 99 per cent effective when taken according to instructions. The ordinary or 'combined' pill is safe to take if the girl is bottle-feeding. There is no truth in the commonly held belief that using birth control pills makes it harder to have babies later on. It is not safe to borrow pills from a sister or friend.

Different contraceptives suit different people, but only condoms protect against pregnancy *and* sexually transmitted diseases.

Avoiding pregnancy

Injections and implants

Some girls find it very hard to remember to take the pill each day. For them, a **contraceptive** injection, or an **implant** placed under the skin of the upper arm, might be more suitable. An injection such as Depo-Provera lasts for twelve weeks and an implant is effective for up to three years. When the implant is taken out, the girl's normal level of **fertility** returns immediately.

IUS and IUD

An **intrauterine system** (IUS) or **device** (IUD) placed in the **womb** is effective for five years or longer, but can be taken out at any time. An IUD is not suitable for a girl who has many partners as it may increase the risk of **sexually transmitted diseases**.

Diaphragm or cap

A **diaphragm** (sometimes called a cap) is a good choice for girls who want to use contraception only when they have sex. The diaphragm is put into the **vagina** a short time before **sexual intercourse** takes place. Because pregnancy and birth change the shape of the vagina, it's necessary to have a new diaphragm fitted by a family planning nurse after the birth of a baby. The diaphragm does not offer protection against sexually transmitted infections as a **condom** does.

See a family planning nurse to learn about using contraceptives.

Natural family planning

Some people have religious objections to contraception, or don't like taking tablets. They prefer natural family planning which can be effective if properly used. Women have to be carefully trained to use this method of contraception which involves examining the **mucus** in the vagina to see whether it is a safe time of the month to have sex.

Talk to friends about what contraceptives they use.

Emergency contraception

There are two methods of emergency contraception which can be used after having unprotected sex.

1. The emergency pill can be obtained from family planning clinics and family doctors. This method must be started within 72 hours of sexual intercourse, the earlier the better.
2. If fitted within five days of intercourse, an IUD will prevent a fertilized egg implanting in the uterus.

In the UK and Australia, contraception is generally available for free from family doctors (**GPs**) and from family planning clinics, young people's clinics and sexual health clinics. Details of how to find contraceptive services are given on pages 52–53.

Information and advice

There are many organizations that provide confidential counselling and help for young people in crisis:

Contacts in the UK

British Agencies for Adoption and Fostering (BAAF)

200 Union Street, London, SE1 0LX
Tel: 020 7593 2000
web site: www.baaf.org.uk
BAAF publishes a useful leaflet called 'Pregnant and Thinking About Adoption'. Also provides information on foster care.

Brook Advisory Centres

Tel: 0800 0815 023
web site: www.brook.org.uk
Brook offers free pregnancy testing. These centres also provide sex advice and **contraception** for young people under 25.

Childline

Tel: 0800 1111
web site: www.childline.org.uk
Childline is a free, 24-hour helpline for children and young people in trouble or danger. The lines can be busy, so keep trying.

Family Planning Association

2–12 Pentonville Road, London, N1 9FP
Freephone: 0845 310 1334 (9am–7pm)
Ring this number to find out where your nearest family planning or sexual health clinic is. Clinics provide services free of charge.

Fathers Direct

Tamarisk House, 37 The Televillage, Crickhowell, NP8 1BP
Tel: 01873 810515
On-line magazine for fathers: www.fathersdirect.com
This is a new organization specifically for fathers of all ages.

Maternity Alliance

45 Beech Street, London, EC2P 2LX
Tel: 020 7588 8582
web site: www.maternityalliance.co.uk
The Alliance provides advice on benefits for pregnant teenagers and teenagers with babies.

National Childbirth Trust (NCT)

Alexandra House, Oldham Terrace, Acton, London W3 6NH
Tel: 0870 444 8707
Breastfeeding information Tel: 0870 444 8708
web site: www.nctpregnancyandbabycare.com
Trained teachers and breastfeeding counsellors offer antenatal classes and breastfeeding support. Breastfeeding services are provided free and antenatal classes are free for those who cannot afford to pay.

Contacts in Australia

Family Planning Australia: National Office

9/114 Maitland Street, Hackett, ACT 2602
Tel: (02) 6230 5255
Fax: (02) 6230 5344
web site: www.fpa.net.au

Kids Helpline

Tel: 1800 55 1800

web site: www.kidshelp.com.au

This is a confidential listening service to help young people with problems. Different states have their own organizations to help parents of all ages.

Family Planning Association of Queensland

100 Alfred Street, Fortitude Valley, QLD 4006

Tel: (07) 3252 5151

Fax: (07) 3854 1277

web site: www.fpq.asn.au

Family Planning Victoria

901 Whitehorse Road, Box Hill, VIC 3128

Tel: (03) 9257 0123

web site: www.fpv.org.au

Family Planning Association of Western Australia

70 Roe Street, Northbridge, WA 6865

Tel: (08) 9227 6177

Fax: (08) 9227 6871

web site: www.fpwa-health.org.au

Further reading

Dear Diary, I'm pregnant: teenagers talk about their pregnancy,

by Annrenee Englander (Editor), Corinne M Wilks. Annick Press, 1997

Pregnancy and parenthood: the views and experiences of young people in public care,

by Judith Corlyon, Christine McGuire. Natl Childrens Bureau, 1999

Teen pregnancy (contemporary issues companion),

by Myra Immell (Editor). Greenhaven Press, 2000

Teens and pregnancy: a hot issue,

by Ann Byers. Enslow Publishers, 2000

Unzipped: everything teenagers want to know about love, sex and each other,

by Bronwyn Donaghy. HarperCollins Publishers, 2000

Glossary

abortion
when doctors bring a pregnancy to an end using drugs or surgery

abusive relationship
when a girl's relative or partner forces her to have sex against her will, or hits, hurts or humiliates her

amniotic fluid
water surrounding the baby in the womb

anaemia
having too few red blood cells; causes tiredness, breathlessness and loss of appetite

asthma
allergic disease which causes breathing difficulties

bladder
where urine collects until you go to the toilet

cervix
neck of the womb which opens during labour so that the baby can be born

circulation
flow of blood around the body

condom
soft, rubber sheath placed over the penis to prevent pregnancy and protect against sexual infections

contraceptive
something that prevents pregnancy

cot death
when a healthy baby suddenly dies for no obvious reason

diabetes
people who have diabetes have too much sugar in their bloodstream

diagnostic test
test that can identify a particular disease

diaphragm
rubber cap, shaped like a saucer, that fits inside the vagina over the opening of the womb

DNA
substance that carries genetic information in living cells

douche
flushing out the vagina with water or other substances

eczema
allergy which makes the skin red, sore and itchy

female condom
soft, plastic pouch which lines the inside of the vagina to prevent the man's sperm reaching the woman's womb during sex

fertility
ability of a woman to conceive a baby

foetus
unborn baby

formula milk
milk made from cow's milk and given to babies who are not breastfed

fostering
caring for a child or young person who is not your own

general anaesthetic
drug to make patients unconscious before surgery

GP
General Practitioner; a doctor who is not a specialist, but offers general medical care

HIV
Human Immunodeficiency Virus; the virus that causes AIDS

hormones
chemical messengers which cause changes in certain parts of the body, especially during pregnancy and labour

implant
contraceptive placed under the woman's skin

injunction
court order requiring a person to do or not to do something

intrauterine device
small copper object put into the womb to prevent pregnancy

intrauterine system
small plastic object put into the womb that releases a chemical to prevent pregnancy

labour
process of giving birth to a baby

lanugo
fine hair covering an unborn baby from the fifth to eighth month of pregnancy

lubricant
any substance that prevents rubbing or friction

miscarriage
when a woman loses a baby during the first 28 weeks of pregnancy

mucus
sticky, jelly-like substance produced by the vagina to keep it moist

multiple sclerosis
disease affecting the nervous system

osteoporosis
disease affecting the bones of the back, pelvis, ribs, arms and legs; common in older women

peer-group
friends most likely to influence someone's behaviour

period
loss of blood from the vagina which women experience monthly from about the age of 12 until 50. Periods stop during pregnancy.

pessary
jelly-like substance that melts when placed in the vagina

placenta
during pregnancy, the placenta (or afterbirth) passes food and oxygen from the mother to the baby; once the baby is born, the body pushes it out of the womb

premature baby
baby who is born before 37 weeks of pregnancy

Rhesus
people whose blood has the Rhesus Factor are 'Rhesus positive'; people who don't have the Rhesus Factor are 'Rhesus negative'

rubella
infection also called German Measles which causes abnormalities in the baby if the mother catches it during the first three months of pregnancy

screening test
test to separate people at low risk of a disease from those at higher risk and who need further tests

sexual intercourse
'having sex' or 'making love'

sexually transmitted disease
diseases such as syphilis, gonorrhoea and HIV caught through having sex with someone who already has the infection

sickle cell disease
disease caused by abnormally shaped red blood cells

spina bifida
condition where the baby's spine is not complete and he or she is born partially paralysed

sterilization
using steam, chemicals or very high temperatures to kill harmful bacteria

thalassaemia
kind of anaemia which sometimes affects people who come from the Mediterranean

thalidomide
drug once given to treat morning sickness, later found to cause serious deformities in babies

toxoplasmosis
infection that can be caught from cats; if a pregnant woman becomes infected, her baby might have brain and eye abnormalities

trimester
pregnancy is divided into first, middle and final trimesters, each lasting three months

ultrasound scan
use of sound technology so that the unborn baby can be seen on a television screen

vaccination
injections to protect against serious infections such as tetanus, diphtheria and rubella

vagina
passage between a woman's legs which the penis enters during sex and which the baby comes down to be born

womb
sometimes called uterus – where the baby grows during the nine months of pregnancy

Index

Titles in the *Need to Know* series include:

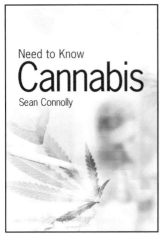

Need to Know
Cannabis
Sean Connolly

Hardback   0 431 09795 X

Need to Know
Eating Disorders
Caroline Warbrick

Hardback   0 431 09799 2

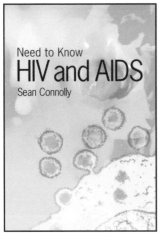

Need to Know
HIV and AIDS
Sean Connolly

Hardback   0 431 09796 8

Need to Know
Sexually Transmitted Diseases
Sean Connolly

Hardback   0 431 09797 6

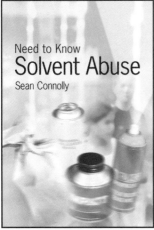

Need to Know
Solvent Abuse
Sean Connolly

Hardback   0 431 09794 1

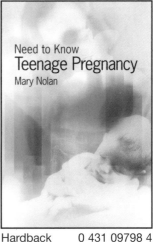

Need to Know
Teenage Pregnancy
Mary Nolan

Hardback   0 431 09798 4

Find out about the other titles in this series on our website www.heinemann.co.uk/library